CHANEL
IN 55 OBJECTS

Published in 2023 by Welbeck,
An imprint of Welbeck Non-Fiction Limited,
part of Welbeck Publishing Group.

Based in London and Sydney
www.welbeckpublishing.com

First published by Welbeck in 2021 as *Chanel Paperscapes*

Text © Emma Baxter-Wright 2021, 2023
Design and layout © Welbeck Non-fiction Limited 2023

A CIP catalogue record for this book is available from the
British Library.

ISBN 978 1 80279 520 2

10 9 8 7 6 5 4 3 2 1

Printed in China

Illustrations: Francesca Waddell / Lipstick of London Ltd

CHANEL
IN 55 OBJECTS

THE ICONIC
DESIGNER THROUGH HER
FINEST CREATIONS

EMMA BAXTER-WRIGHT

WELBECK

CONTENTS

1
GABRIELLE "COCO" CHANEL

BORN: 19 AUGUST 1883
DIED: 10 JANUARY 1971
CREATED: A CONTEMPORARY WARDROBE FOR
TWENTIETH-CENTURY WOMEN
LEGACY: LIBERATED THE FEMALE BODY

The meteoric rags-to-riches story that saw Gabrielle "Coco" Chanel elevated from her humble beginnings in Saumur to become one of the most successful women in the world is a complex narrative, shaped by personal sacrifice and tragedy.

Once described as "the exterminating angel of nineteenth-century style", Chanel led a revolution in womenswear which rejected the oppressive constraints of male-dominated couture, in favour of physical freedom and understated elegance. She grasped every opportunity that life presented, and the decisions she made were all informed by her personal circumstances. Impulsive and instinctive, she believed passionately that a newfound shift toward simplicity would facilitate the evolving role of women in a changing world.

Renowned as a great beauty with a unique personality, Chanel was as skilful at reinventing the details of her sorrowful origins as she was in reshaping the future landscape of fashion. Success came rapidly and the House of Chanel established a global legacy built around a lexicon of must-have items, which still resonates today: the Little Black Dress, the visual extravagance of costume jewellery, the perfect symmetry of an unstructured suit, and Chanel Nº5, the best-selling perfume ever invented.

Fame and fortune were not compensation enough for a woman who needed love, and later in life, without marriage or a family, Chanel became increasingly isolated – but as friends and lovers came and went, her commitment to the success of her business remained a constant in her life.

2
AUBAZINE ABBEY

DATE: FOUNDED IN 1134
LOCATION: CORRÈZE VALLEY, SOUTH
CENTRAL FRANCE
SIGNIFICANCE: AESTHETIC INSPIRATION
FOR SIGNATURE EMBLEMS

With the premature death of her 32-year-old mother Eugénie Jeanne Devolle, Chanel and her surviving siblings, two sisters and two brothers (Julia-Berthe, Antoinette, Alphonse and Lucien) were dependent on the wayward care of their pedlar father, Henri-Albert Chanel. Unwilling or unable to cope, he shrugged off the responsibilities of fatherhood by abandoning his three daughters to a convent orphanage in nearby Aubazine and offloading his young sons as child labourers.

Life at the twelfth-century Cistercian monastery and abbey was to have a profound effect on Chanel, who spent part of her childhood here, followed by a lifetime reinventing her childhood, deliberately choosing never to mention the word "orphanage". The influence of this formative experience can be found as a recurring theme in much of Chanel's iconography; the atmosphere of religious austerity, and the simple ceremonial uniforms, had a significant impact. The intricate patterns of the stained-glass windows in the Cistercian abbey are thought to have provided inspiration for her iconic double C logo, while the complex graphic mosaics on the floor inspired crosses and star-shaped jewellery. The simple black and white nun's habit, the rosary beads and the chain belts can be traced through Chanel's repeated use of monotone, long ropes of pearls and her love of chains.

In 1929 she insisted the architect designing her new house in the south of France visit the abbey, to replicate the impressive staircase of the convent, another important indication of the aesthetic influences of her early life.

3
CABARET

DATE: 1902
LOCATION: MOULINS
VENUE: OPEN-AIR PAVILION WHERE CHANEL
MADE HER SINGING DEBUT
SIGNIFICANCE: ACQUIRED THE NICKNAME "COCO"

From a very early age Chanel was determined to make something of her life, having endured a wretched childhood, overshadowed by her mother's untimely death and her father's decision to abandon his girls to the orphanage at Aubazine.

Searching for recognition and the love she felt deprived of by the humble circumstances of her upbringing, Chanel had early ambitions to become a performer, and considered both singing and dancing as a possible future career. In the garrison town of Moulins, about 240 km (150 miles) from Paris, Chanel made her debut at the age of almost 20 as a singer at La Rotonde, a café pavilion popular with the aristocratic regiment of the 10th Chasseurs. Despite a rather weak singing voice, Chanel would entertain the audience in-between the star acts of the cabaret, being allowed to keep the money thrown into a hat by the wealthy young officers, who appreciated her enthusiastic performance and charm. Her vaudeville repertoire was limited to two catchy songs: 'Qui Qu' a Vu Coco' a simple ditty about a Parisian lady who had lost her little puppy dog, and 'Ko-Ko-Ri-Ko'. With dark flashing eyes, and mischievous looks, she proved popular with the audience made up mostly of prosperous gentleman, who called out for "la petite Coco" to entertain them.

Present in the audience at La Rotonde was Étienne Balsan, an admirer who would go on to help Chanel achieve success, while the nickname "Coco" would endure throughout her life, utilized in the iconic double C logo that became synonymous with her brand of understated elegance.

4
THE EQUESTRIENNE

DATE: 1905

PLACE: CHATEAU DE ROYALLIEU

SIGNIFICANCE: APPROPRIATION
OF MALE WARDROBE

Étienne Balsan loved women and horses, and when Chanel moved to live with him in her 20s, she too discovered pleasure in the solitude of the stables, among the thoroughbreds he trained.

Spending time with the stable lads and riding every day in jodhpurs and tweed hacking jackets bought from the men's tailor in La Croix Saint Ouen, Chanel became an accomplished horsewoman, riding astride like a man and sliding off over the horse's tail to dismount. Among the colourful courtesans who often stayed at the chateau, ostentatiously dressed in lavish outfits, Chanel felt like an outsider, and visually differentiated herself by choosing to dress down in a style more reminiscent of a young boy – flat shoes, cropped trousers and a plain white shirt, decorated with a simple black ribbon at the neck. This first example of appropriation – taking practical pieces from a male wardrobe to reinvent them for women in a changing society – would become a signature style for Chanel, who was always influenced by the sporting attire of the men in her life.

Horses remained a lifelong passion for Chanel, who could often be found watching the races at Longchamp, and years later she utilized the simplicity of quilting taken from the stable boys' working jackets to create the distinctive matelassé, diamond-shaped topstitching on her famous 2.55 handbag. The understated beauty of the polished leather harness, shiny metal stirrup irons and bridle bits worn by the horses, are also believed to have been the main source of inspiration for the handbag's metal strap interlaced with leather.

5

ARTHUR "BOY" CAPEL

DATE: BORN 1881, DIED 22 DECEMBER 1919 IN AN
AUTOMOBILE ACCIDENT
OCCUPATION: INDUSTRIALIST, POLO PLAYER
SIGNIFICANCE: FINANCIAL SPONSOR,
AND LOVE OF HER LIFE

The years Chanel spent with Boy Capel were almost certainly the happiest of her life. His unexpected death in a tragic car accident at the age of 38 left her bereft and broken. Many years later, she told the author Paul Morand, "In losing Capel I lost everything. He left a void in me that the years have not filled."

As a friend of Étienne Balsan, Capel was a frequent weekend guest at the chateau, where Chanel fell for him and impulsively followed him back to Paris, leaving a note for Balsan that read simply: "Forgive me, but I love him."

An educated Englishman with wealth acquired from coal mines in Newcastle, Capel was captivated by Chanel, believed in her potential to make a career as a modiste, and nurtured her cultural development by advising her which books to read and furniture to collect. Chanel lived with Capel in Paris, but understood he had other distractions, and marriage was out of the question due to her lack of social status. She was unaware that her first retail ventures were bankrolled by Capel's securities, and worked tirelessly to repay the debt in record time when she found out, never wanting to be thought of as a kept woman. When her business proved successful, he suggested expansion, recommending the locations for a shop in Deauville in 1912 and Biarritz in 1915.

When Capel married the Honourable Diana Wyndham in 1918, Chanel was devastated, though greater tragedy was to come when he was killed in a fatal accident almost two years later.

6
THE MODISTE

DATE: 1910
LOCATION: 21 RUE CAMBON, PARIS
FINANCED BY: BOY CAPEL
ENDORSED BY: WEALTHY FRIENDS OF ÉTIENNE
BALSAN

Holidays away from the orphanage were sometimes spent with her paternal grandparents, where Chanel would often sit at the kitchen table with her Aunt Louise and Aunt Adrienne (the youngest of 19 siblings on her father's side) and stitch plain ribbons on to simple hats and bonnets. Later, when she moved to live with Étienne Balsan at his estate Chateau de Royallieu, she made further attempts to create her own understated style of millinery, determined to stand apart from the ostentatious luxury of the Belle Époque. Rejecting the fancy feather trimmings, ornate ribbons and frilly bows that defined popular fashion, Chanel instinctively knew that extravagant things didn't suit her.

Her pared-down hats were admired by the bohemian crowd of courtesans and actresses who were regular visitors at the chateau, and soon they were commissioning her to make bespoke hats for them. Not cut out for a life of idleness, Chanel was amused to discover that the more she charged her wealthy customers, the more they were willing to pay, and that a basic boater bought for pennies at Galeries Lafayette could be decorated with a simple bow and sold on for a profit.

Selling firstly from Balsan's studio apartment in Boulevard Malesherbes, and then later expanding to a commercial property on rue Cambon, Chanel opened her first shop, Chanel Modes, in 1910, with the stipulation from the landlord that she was to supply only millinery and not clothes. When Gabrielle Dorziat wore her hats on stage in 1912 in the play *Bel Ami*, Chanel received rave reviews from the fashion magazine *Journal des Modes*.

7
DEAUVILLE

DATE: 1912

LOCATION: FASHIONABLE SEASIDE RESORT
ON THE NORTH COAST OF FRANCE

SIGNIFICANCE: SOLD CLOTHES AND MILLINERY

INNOVATION: NAUTICAL CHIC

As a couturière who sought to offer women freedom of choice and ease of movement, Chanel was very much her own best example. Slim and sporty, she spent hours at the beach, playing tennis and swimming in the sparkling waters of the French coastal resorts she visited with Boy Capel.

With his encouragement and financial sponsorship, Chanel opened her first boutique in Deauville, a place that appealed to her because it attracted a wealthy crowd of visitors and was also home to a world-famous racetrack. The shop itself, situated on rue Gontaut-Biron, championed a new style of comfortable dressing for women. Now in addition to elegant hats, she offered clothing that was unrestrictive – and much better suited to a more relaxed lifestyle at the seaside. Chanel's early prototypes of modernism set a template that was to become recognized the world over, as the loose, belted cardigans and fluid skirts and trousers she produced evolved into her signature pieces. She took the standard uniform of the Normandy fishermen she saw on the quayside each day and reinvented it with contemporary women in mind, producing casual striped jersey sweaters and wide loose trousers.

Quick to recognize the importance of creating publicity for her new venture, she dressed her beautiful aunt Adrienne and her younger sister Antoinette in the casually elegant pieces she was producing. Wandering the boardwalk each day in a different outfit, they exemplified a new style of chic, which resonated with the women holidaying in Deauville, who asked them where they bought their clothes.

8
BEACHWEAR

DATE: 1913–15
LOCATION: DEAUVILLE AND BIARRITZ
FABRIC: KNITTED JERSEY
SIGNIFICANCE: EMANCIPATION OF WOMENSWEAR

Practical sportswear was an early innovation of Chanel, who felt that women should be offered the same freedom as men, in the form of unrestrictive clothing that allowed ease of movement and comfort. Chanel loved outdoor activity – she rode horses, played tennis and golf, and swam in the ocean – and as with so much of her creativity, it was the desire for stylish simplicity in her own life which inspired the commercial designs that she offered to others. From her boutique in the coastal resort of Deauville, Chanel provided a ground-breaking collection of co-ordinated jersey separates, perfect for a casual beach wardrobe: long fluid cardigan jackets, casual skirts and simple tops inspired by workwear. Chanel also popularized sunbathing, promoting the idea of a healthy glow at a time when having porcelain skin was a sign of class and beauty.

The striped bathing suits she produced in the 1920s – typically knee-length shorts and tank-top vests – were considered racy compared to the Victorian bloomers worn at the turn of the century, and although knitted jersey was heavy to swim in, these costumes pioneered the idea of exposure to cultivate a suntan. Chanel appeared in her own beach pyjamas as early as 1918, instigating another trend that chic society women wanted to copy. The elegant, wide-legged trousers, often made from linen or satin, were perfect beach attire and could be seen on the most glamorous women in the upmarket resorts of the French Riviera from the 1920s onward.

9
BIARRITZ COUTURE HOUSE

DATE: 1915
BUILDING: TURRETED, FOUR-STOREY VILLA
LOCATION: OPPOSITE THE BEACH AND THE CASINO
FASHION MOMENT: FIRST RANGE OF COUTURE
CLOTHES

Despite the upheaval of the First World War, Boy Capel, now signed up as a captain in the British army, was able to take Chanel away for a weekend break in 1915 to the Hotel du Palais in the Basque town of Biarritz. Situated close to the border of neutral Spain and seemingly unaffected by the

war, it was populated with wealthy European aristocracy and minor royalty, and would, suggested Capel, be a perfect location to expand the business.

Chanel found an impressive mansion between the beach and the casino, which gave her the opportunity to open her first couture shop, to cater to a cosmopolitan audience desperate to indulge in some retail therapy as a means of distraction. Women's lives were changing radically, and the unpredictable turmoil of war resulted in fabric shortages, but Chanel was inventive, realizing that these new circumstances required a different type of luxury. Soft knitted jersey was used to make fashionable sporty couture, simple tunic dresses, cardigans, culotte trousers and tank tops. Although not always easy to work with, the fabric had a beautiful drape and was comfortable to wear.

After years of stiff restrictive clothing, Chanel offered an unstructured fluidity that became the height of fashion: orders flooded in, from the Spanish court and from members of the Russian aristocracy who had been exiled to Biarritz. Chanel brought her sister Antoinette down from Paris to help run the shop, and by the end of the war her business was so successful she employed a staff of 300 to cope with demand.

10
JERSEY

DATE: 1916
SUPPLIER: JEAN RODIER
CATALYST: FABRIC SHORTAGES DUE
TO THE FIRST WORLD WAR
SIGNIFICANCE: REJECTION OF THE CORSET

During the war, extravagant outfits seemed at odds with the difficult times, and to Chanel it seemed logical that fashion needed a radical overhaul. With many fabrics hard to come by, she seized the opportunity to work with the only fabrics that *were* available. As she said later to Paul Morand, "unwittingly I offered simplicity, comfort and neatness", turning knitted jersey, for the first time, into the height of fashion.

Early success came when Chanel put on an oversized man's sweater in Deauville because she was cold, tying a loose scarf around the waist and creating an ultra-modern casual "dress". At that time, jersey was not considered suitable either for women or for dresses, because it was a fabric used only for men's clothing – for underwear, sports sweaters or schoolboy blazers. Chanel's inventive use of the fluid fabric, first for beachwear and then cut into comfortable day and evening wear that could be worn without a corset, proved to be a revolutionary moment in fashion history.

Chanel bought a cheap job lot of jersey from Jean Rodier, a leading manufacturer who was unable to shift his stock because it was too scratchy to be used for underwear. Chanel knew that the muted colours and soft properties of the fabric would work well as hip-length cardigan jackets, straight tunics and sailor blouses – clothes designed for a generation of women made slimmer by food rationing, who required a new style of dressing. With a growing reputation for making elegant sports clothes that skimmed the uncorseted figure and were commercially successful, *Vogue* declared: "Everything she does makes news."

11

THE BOB

DATE: 1917

CATALYST: FEMALE EMANCIPATION

CIRCUMSTANCE: A FORTUITOUS ACCIDENT

INSPIRED BY: COLETTE AND AVANT-GARDE

DANCER CARYATHIS

The war years upended life for wealthy women in society and escalated the advancement of female liberation. Without a team of maids to help them dress and style their hair, women looked for an easier way to present themselves, more in tune with the newfound opportunities they were experiencing. They no longer had to seek permission to go out without a chaperone, and when the automobile replaced the horse and cart, the need for freedom of movement with practical skirts of a shorter length became paramount.

Chanel was at the forefront of this fashionable revolution and represented a new type of youthful modernism, which women wanted to emulate. She first cut her hair in 1917, telling Paul Morand in an interview in 1945 that the impetus to do so was "Because it annoys me." Later she recounted a different story to her close friend Claude Delay, explaining the decision to cut her waist-length hair, which she usually wore wrapped in braids around her head, was the result of an accident. Getting ready for a night out at the opera, Chanel fiddled with the pilot light in the bathroom – and a mini explosion singed her hair, forcing her to cut each individual braid off. The explosive gas also marked her white dress with soot. Undeterred, Chanel hurriedly changed and set off that night in a simple black dress, revealing for the first time her new short bob. Admired by everyone at the opera who talked about the beauty of her neck, Chanel's impulsive decision helped facilitate the growing trend for women to adopt a boyish hairstyle.

12

MISIA SERT

DATE: 1917

PROFESSION: GIFTED PIANIST, ARTIST'S MUSE
AND PHILANTHROPIST

RELATIONSHIP: COMPETITIVE FRIENDSHIP

SIGNIFICANCE: INTRODUCED CHANEL TO ALL THE
LEADING ARTISTS IN PARIS

"Always bored, but never boring" is how Chanel described her closest female friend, Misia Sert, who was to have an enduring influence on the couturière during their complex, 30-year relationship.

Maria Zofia Olga Zenajda Godebska was born near St Petersburg in 1872, and became an intriguing patron of the artists, musicians and writers who populated Paris in the early years of the twentieth century, immortalized as a great beauty in the works of Bonnard, Vuillard, Toulouse-Lautrec and Renoir. Intrigued by Chanel when they met at a dinner party given by the actress Cécile Sorel in 1917, Sert complimented her at the end of the evening on the velvet coat she wore and was charmed when Chanel spontaneously gave it to her. Consequently, Sert and her future third husband José María Sert were to become loyal supporters of Chanel throughout the turbulent years ahead.

Invited to join them on their honeymoon in Italy, Chanel overheard a private conversation concerning the financial hardship of Sergei Diaghilev's ballet company and made it her business to secretly offer the 300,000 francs needed to stage a revival of *Le Sacre du Printemps (The Rite of Spring)*, on condition that the gift was not mentioned to Sert.

Acceptance into the arts world resulted in Chanel collaborating with Jean Cocteau and Pablo Picasso, giving rise to petty jealousies between the women, as Sert liked to control and manipulate the people around her. Despite ongoing squabbles in their relationship, Chanel personally took care of the funeral arrangements for her friend when she died in 1950.

13

TROUSERS

DATE: 1918
LOCATION: DEAUVILLE, BIARRITZ
AND VENICE
FABRIC: JERSEY, RAW SILK, LINEN

Much of Chanel's instincts for innovative design came from her own desire to dress in a way that was practical and devoid of unnecessary decorative clutter.

During the war effort many women were required to work for the first time in their lives and needed to wear sturdy, functional uniforms, including trousers, to perform practical tasks. Such workwear was not considered appropriate or fashionable for women, but Chanel helped change the mindset about clothes that were comfortable and easy, redefining what could and should be part of a contemporary dress code. During extended German bombing raids on Paris, women had to take refuge in basement shelters and needed something easy to throw on. Throughout her career Chanel proved to be a quick-minded opportunist, who was adept at providing stylish solutions, and on this occasion she created a demand for men's jersey pyjamas, sold at high-fashion prices from her shop in rue Cambon.

From the 1920s onward, Chanel popularized what she called "pyjamas for the beach", based on the prototype of the male pyjama, but produced in a range of luxurious fabrics. Often photographed at the seaside in her own version of white yachting trousers, these were not considered acceptable for other social occasions until years later.

14
FUR

DATE: 1918
CATALYST: FUEL SHORTAGES FOR HEATING
ORIGIN: RABBIT
USED FOR: CUFFS, HATS, COLLARS

During the war years couturiers learnt to be inventive, as so many of the materials they would normally work with were in short supply.

Life in Paris was gloomy as well as freezing cold, and the price of coal rocketed (boosting Boy Capel's wealth enormously) while women turned to fur for a practical and glamorous means of keeping themselves warm. Without international imports available, the luxurious pelts that Chanel would have preferred to use, such as chinchilla bought from South America or sable from Russia, were simply not an option. Chanel was a quick-thinking problem-solver, who found a practical solution by swapping expensive pelts with much cheaper alternatives, what she called "the humblest of hides". She substituted expensive skins for rabbit fur, decoratively cut into narrow bands to adorn the hem and collar of her slim jersey outfits, winning praise from *Vogue,* who wrote: "Chanel's fur-trimmed jersey dresses are making her a fortune."

For women who couldn't afford an entire leopard-skin coat, accessories such as hats, muffs, collars, gloves and cuffs trimmed with pieces of fur were the height of fashion, although they were advised not to enquire too closely as to exactly which animal had produced the skins. Although not favoured by Chanel, monkey fur, recognized for its distinctive dark colour and hair-like shaggy texture, was commonly used as a decorative trim for smaller items at this time by other designers such as Elsa Schiaparelli.

15

31 RUE CAMBON

LOCATION: 1ST ARRONDISSEMENT, PARIS
DATE: EIGHTEENTH CENTURY
ARCHITECTURAL STYLE: CLASSICAL
FLOORS: SIX

The 1st arrondissement in Paris, known colloquially in French as *premier*, is the heart of the City of Light, one of the oldest parts of the French capital and home to some of the most celebrated and beautiful buildings in Paris, including the Louvre and the Tuileries Garden. One street in particular is home to possibly the chicest landmark of all, 31 rue Cambon, the headquarters for the House of Chanel.

Chanel's boutiques in Deauville (1912) and Biarritz (1915) had both flourished during the First World War, under the patronage of wealthy women seeking refuge at the seaside, and by 1918 she was doing so well financially that she was able to expand her business. Moving down the road from her original premises at 21 rue Cambon, Chanel found an impressive six-storey building at number 31, and the town-house building still remains as the centre of operations for the House of Chanel.

Acquiring this substantial property, Chanel was as innovative as ever, turning the building into a contemporary holistic haute couture house and boutique, selling not only her latest garments and millinery but also providing customers with accessories, perfume, jewellery and her newly launched beauty products. Chanel herself occupied an apartment above the haute couture salons, although she never slept there, always returning to her suite across the road at The Ritz. The apartment at 31 rue Cambon has been preserved exactly as Chanel created it, with her famous Chinese lacquer screens, elegant sofas and beautiful antique furniture, an example of classical elegance, much like the designs of the House of Chanel. The apartment as well as the mirrored staircase were listed in 2013 by the Ministry of Culture as historical monuments, in recognition of their national significance.

<u>16</u>
SCISSORS

DATE: 1919
SIGNIFICANCE: SCISSORS DISPLAYED AS ARTEFACTS
LOCATION: BEDSIDE TABLE AT THE RITZ AND
HER RUE CAMBON APARTMENT
WORN: DAILY, AROUND CHANEL'S NECK

Hard at work in the studio at rue Cambon each day, Chanel brandished her trusted scissors, the most crucial part of her toolkit, like another designer would express their ideas with a 2B pencil. She did not draw out any of her designs on paper but worked directly with fabric, first from a cotton toile, then later with the specific materials she had chosen. Always a perfectionist, Chanel would spend hours working with the house

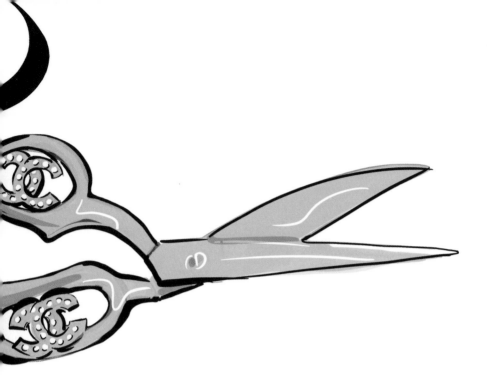

mannequins, striving to create a flawless fit for the sleeve head, cigarette suspended between her crimson lips, scissors dangling on a ribbon around her neck. She had "special collection scissors" threaded on to tape and worn like a medallion, but also kept silver gilt scissors and beautifully crafted, folding Nogent scissors laid out on her coromandel tables in her apartment.

In conversation with her great friend Claude Delay, Chanel spoke of the significance of her cutting tools, expressing a wish that if she *were* to have a family crest, it would certainly include a symbolic pair of scissors. Without formal training, Chanel worked instinctively, using her fingers to flatten unsightly folds and her scissors to snip away excess cloth, working rapidly, sculpting the fabric into submission and looking for an understated elegance in everything she produced. At the end of a long day, Madame Raymonde, who worked with Chanel in her studio, would retrieve the tape with the scissors from around Mademoiselle's neck, and place them ready for the next day's duties, part of a disciplined work ritual that Chanel adhered to throughout her life.

17
VENICE

❀

DATE: 1920
WITH: MISIA AND JOSÉ MARÍA SERT
CULTURAL EDUCATION: ITALIAN ART AND
ARCHITECTURE OF THE CITY
SIGNIFICANCE: INTRODUCTION TO SERGEI DIAGHILEV

In an extraordinary gesture of friendship, Chanel's friends Misia and José María Sert insisted that she join them on their grand honeymoon tour of Italy, to help distract her from the grief of losing Boy Capel. Cruising along the Adriatic coast, they stopped first at Venice, where Chanel was enthralled by the sheer beauty of this historical city built on water.

José "Jojo" Sert was a larger-than-life Catalan artist, described by Paul Morand in *The Allure of Chanel* as "an ideal travelling companion, always in a good mood", who took great pleasure in educating Chanel about the stunning juxtaposition of architectural styles she was witnessing for the first time. Behind the crumbling facades of the Venetian palazzos, he pointed out the distinction between the Byzantine, Gothic and Renaissance architecture, introduced her to the hidden secrets of the city, and the breathtaking colours found in works of art by Tintoretto and Titian, viewed in the churches for which the paintings were originally commissioned. Chanel was impressed at the scale of the grand altarpiece crosses, and the golden mosaics that covered the walls of St Mark's Basilica, taking much of what she saw as inspiration for future work.

Venice held a special place in Chanel's life and she would return many times, as part of a fashionable crowd who partied on the lido, or sipped cocktails at Caffè Florian in St Mark's Square, looking elegant in white linen. It was on this honeymoon trip that Misia first introduced Chanel to the great Russian impresario, founder and artistic director of the Ballets Russes, Sergei Diaghilev, with whom she would go on to have many successful collaborations.

18

THE LION

DATE: 19 AUGUST 1883
SOURCE: LEO, HER ASTROLOGICAL SIGN
SIGNIFICANCE: INFLUENCED IMPORTANT
DECISIONS IN HER LIFE
UTILIZED: LION'S HEAD WAS EMBOSSED ON TO
GILT BUTTONS

The astrological signs of the zodiac, ritualistic symbols and strange superstitious beliefs all played a significant role in the way Chanel conducted her life, and in many of the intuitive business decisions she took. She was a firm believer in numerology, kept good luck talismans, and was fascinated by the constellations, once admitting: "I love everything that's up high; the sky, the moon and I believe in the stars."

Born under the sign of the lion, the fifth astrological sign of the zodiac, Chanel clung to the symbolism of her birth sign, using both the number five and the emblem of Leo to great effect in her creative work.

In desolation, after the tragedy of Boy Capel's accident, Chanel travelled to Venice with her friends Misia and José María Sert, and was captivated by the magnificent sculpture of a winged lion that stands proudly overlooking St Mark's Square, protecting the city. Taking solace from the iconography of the majestic lion which she saw all over Venice – on door knockers, built into the facade of the Arsenale and on the Venetian flag – Chanel found inner strength and slowly started to rebuild her shattered confidence. Back in her apartment in Paris, Chanel surrounded herself with multiple sculptural lions, of different proportions, which all served to protect her and symbolized the courage she needed to continue. She incorporated the lion's head in many of her collections, embossed on to the heavy gilt buttons she loved, and also in decorative brooches.

19

BALLETS RUSSES

FOUNDED: 1909
LOCATION: PARIS
SIGNIFICANCE: FRIENDSHIP AND SPONSORSHIP
OF SERGEI DIAGHILEV
PROFESSIONAL INVOLVEMENT: COSTUME DESIGN
FOR THE BALLET

When the great artistic impresario Sergei Diaghilev brought his Russian troupe of dancers to Paris in the early years of the twentieth century, the whole city fell under his magical spell. The Ballets Russes caused a sensation, showcasing a series of avant-garde productions that featured a new style of assertive performance.

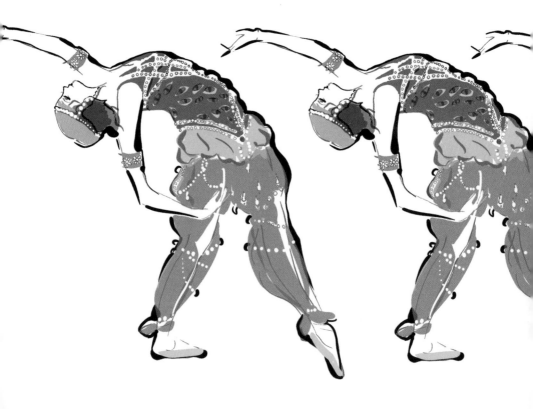

The flamboyant Russian was a friend of Misia Sert and was introduced to Chanel in 1920. After cutting his ties with St Petersburg, he had settled in Paris with his company, which performed throughout Europe, but despite critical acclaim and significant success financial disaster regularly loomed. Chanel's patronage – a secret gift of 300,000 francs which allowed Diaghilev to restage *The Rite of Spring* – sealed a lifelong friendship that also saw her collaborating with his company on many occasions as a costume designer.

His experimental productions encompassed dance, music, poetry and sculpture, which appealed to Chanel who loved the audacity of his creative vision because it mirrored her own desire to innovate and subvert. Through his friendship, Chanel was now accepted as part of an artistic team that included Cocteau, Picasso, Braque, Stravinsky and Satie. As her stature and wealth grew, she remained a loyal and generous friend to Diaghilev, hosting parties for him throughout his career, and finally rushing to his bedside when he was gravely ill in Venice. Diaghilev died on Chanel's 46th birthday, 19 August 1929. Chanel and Misia Sert accompanied the funeral gondola to the island of San Michele, Venice's cemetery island, both dressed in white, as he had requested. Chanel paid for all the funeral expenses.

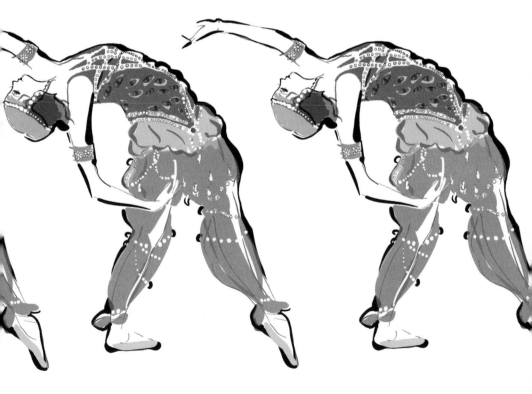

Les Epaves du Ciel

20
PIERRE REVERDY

DATE: 1920

PROFESSION: EXISTENTIAL POET

SIGNIFICANCE: ENCOURAGED CHANEL TO WRITE
HER APHORISMS

Of the many men that Chanel became involved with during the course of her lifetime, the married French poet Pierre Reverdy was perhaps the most intriguing.

Introduced by Misia Sert in 1920, Reverdy was part of the artistic Montmartre crowd that included Max Jacob, Pablo Picasso and Georges Braque, and though he did not in any way conform to her usual type, the attraction between them was instantaneous. Despite the contradictions of this intensely religious man, who published volumes of emotionally stark poetry, and publicly shunned the superficial excesses of high society while sharing Chanel's lavish home on the rue du Faubourg Saint-Honoré and accepting financial support, their bond was profound. Reverdy's dedication to spiritual truth connected with Chanel's inner child, stirring memories of the monastic austerity of her youth. He dedicated his manuscripts to her, wrote notes detailing the books she should read, and encouraged her own writing.

When French *Vogue* asked Chanel to submit her thoughts on her business, she responded with a collection of witty observations, an exercise she was asked to repeat many times over for magazines around the world. Her famous "Chanelisms", which included her forthright opinions on fashion, love and life, were applauded for their concise style and wit, succinct soundbites that Reverdy almost certainly helped to compose. In 1926 Reverdy decided to retreat from the world and commit to a life of solitude in a Benedictine abbey in Sarthe. Chanel remained friends with him for 40 years, knowing that whenever life hit a bumpy patch she could turn to him for support.

21

PEARLS

DATE: 1920
SOURCE: GIFTED BY LOVERS
SIGNIFICANCE: POPULARIZED COSTUME JEWELLERY
LEGACY: A SIGNATURE FOR THE HOUSE OF CHANEL

At the height of her success Chanel was rarely seen without numerous strands of pearls, slung decoratively around her neck, which she believed to be a symbol of good luck. She loved the luminosity of the iridescent gems, the way they enhanced and highlighted her tanned skin, and the visual dynamic they created when worn with her favourite colour – black.

Delighted with the numerous precious items she was gifted by her wealthy admirers, Chanel could see the universal appeal of the pearl necklace but also that these costly gems would be beyond the budgets of most women. She decided to create faux pearl necklaces for her clients, enabling them to buy stunning jewellery for themselves. Strung into oversized ropes that were designed to be worn as eye-catching statement jewels, these playful costume pearls would become a trademark of both Chanel and her brand.

Adopting an understated style of elegance in terms of the clothes she wore, Chanel often adorned herself with stunning pieces of eye-catching jewellery; decorative brooches, enamel cuffs and multiple stands of pearls ensured Chanel positively rattled as she moved. She eschewed the idea that jewellery should be saved for glamorous occasions, wearing her pearls over the Argyll sweaters she wore for hunting, and commenting on how marvellous jewellery looks when worn on sun-bronzed skin. "A very white earring on the lobe of a well-tanned ear delights me," she told Paul Morand. Starting a trend that was emulated by all her wealthy customers, Chanel herself very often mixed affordable paste with valuable gemstones.

22
THE CAMELLIA

DATE: 1920s
SOURCE: *LA DAME AUX CAMÉLIAS* BY ALEXANDRE DUMAS
SIGNIFICANCE: ETERNAL LOVE
LEGACY: A SIGNATURE FOR THE HOUSE OF CHANEL

While the overall aesthetic of Chanel's design ethos was pared-down minimalism, she excelled in adding provocative touches that became instantly recognizable as house signatures for her brand. The white camellia was just one of the essential motifs Chanel favoured as a recurring symbol in her work, finding novel ways to reinvent the flower, whether as a decorative touch or incorporated into complex prints.

The trend for foppish young dandies of the 1920s to wear a camellia in their buttonhole originated from the play *La Dame aux Camélias (The Lady of the Camellias)*, adapted by Alexandre Dumas from his novel of the same name, which was a hit in Parisian society in 1852, and later brought great success for Greta Garbo in the 1936 Hollywood film, *Camille*. Chanel adopted the white camellia, known as the Japanese rose and said to represent long-lasting love, into her collections from the 1920s onward. With an abundance of tightly packed petals, and almost perfectly symmetrical in shape, the exotic camellia was also scentless, another reason for Chanel to choose it, ensuring it could not compete with the aroma of N°5.

Drawn to the visual dynamic of monochrome, Chanel used the white flower to great effect, often placing it against her favourite colour black. The camellia might offer a decorative corsage, be added to the crown of a simple boater or pinned to the lapel of a suit jacket. By the 1930s Chanel was creating stylized prints of the flower on fabric, and by 1938 the atelier of Maison Gripoix had created a delicate glass necklace based on the perfect bloom.

23

ERNEST BEAUX

DATE: 1920

PROFESSION: RUSSIAN-BORN PERFUMER

SIGNIFICANCE: ASSISTED CHANEL IN THE
CREATION OF CHANEL N°5

There was a time when Chanel was heavily influenced by the romantic charm of all things Slavic. She was friends with Igor Stravinsky and Sergei Diaghilev, had a love affair with the Grand Duke Dmitri Pavlovich, and produced collections based on traditional Russian peasant blouses called *roubachkas*.

Introduced to the French Ernest Beaux, a charismatic 40-year-old who had spent his formative years in St Petersburg and worked for the Russian perfume house A Rallet & Co in Moscow, Chanel embarked on a project that was to provide her with financial wealth beyond anything she could have imagined. Ernest Beaux had also been a soldier, honoured by the French with the Croix de Guerre and the Légion d'Honneur for his activity during the First World War, and by the British with the Military Cross for his work as a counter-intelligence officer. In 1919 he set up his perfume factory in the hilltop town of Grasse on the Riviera, where he was introduced to Chanel. The Parisian couturière was very sure of what she wanted when she approached Beaux, and worked hard alongside him at his laboratory each day, impressing him with her extraordinary sense of smell. Using natural ingredients combined with modern chemical compounds called aldehydes to stabilize the formula, Beaux developed what was to become the most famous perfume in the world.

Initially just 100 bottles of Chanel N°5 were produced, to be given as Christmas presents to loyal customers, but the success of the perfume exceeded all expectations. When Les Parfums Chanel was created in 1924, Beaux was hired as the Chief Perfumer.

24

CHANEL N°5

DATE: 1921
CREATED BY: GABRIELLE CHANEL / ERNEST BEAUX
FRAGRANCE: MAY ROSE, JASMINE, YLANG YLANG AND
SANTAL
WORN BY: CATHERINE DENEUVE, MARILYN MONROE

In the summer of 1920, Chanel, determined to create a perfume unlike
any of the popular floral fragrances already available, was introduced to
the eminent Russian-born, French perfumer Ernest Beaux by her aristocratic
lover the Grand Duke Dmitri Pavlovich. At Beaux's headquarters in Grasse,
a small town in southern Provence known as the world's perfume capital,

Chanel worked alongside the perfumer, who had recently introduced synthetic acetates and aldehydes into his formulas to enhance and prolong the subtle odours of natural ingredients. With an acute sense of smell and strong views on the subject – she often quoted the poet Paul Valéry: "A woman who doesn't wear perfume has no future" – Chanel was absolutely certain of what she did not want in her fragrance. Presented with a series of numbered sample vials to test, she chose bottle number five, dismissing Beaux's objections that the fragrance contained more than 80 different ingredients, including neroli, May rose and a high proportion of costly jasmine. To his objection that it would be prohibitively extravagant to produce, Chanel replied, "I want to make the most expensive perfume in the world." Presented in a clear, pharmaceutical style, modernist glass bottle, and radically labelled "N°5", the perfume was first sold through her boutiques the following year, quickly becoming the most successful perfume in the world.

In the 1950s, the glamorous Hollywood screen star Marilyn Monroe was quoted as saying she only ever wore Chanel N°5 in bed, a comment that sent worldwide sales skyrocketing.

25

BAROQUE

DATE: 1921
VENUE: 31 RUE CAMBON
CATALYST: TRIP TO VENICE, 1920
SIGNIFICANCE: ORNATE INTERIORS,
MINIMALIST FASHION

In complete contrast to the understated minimalism that Chanel championed in her contemporary wardrobe for women, the apartment at 31 rue Cambon, where she lived above the haute-couture fitting rooms, was a treasure trove of glittering artefacts. Visitors to Mademoiselle's spacious living quarters were welcomed at the front door by two life-size Renaissance Venetian statues who graciously showed the way in, welcoming guests to rooms that dazzled the eye with an abundance of visually stunning objets d'art, juxtaposed in a style that reflected the originality of their mistress.

Poorly educated as a child, Chanel had filled in the gaps of her knowledge of art, music and literature, encouraged by her close friends Misia and José María Sert, who also took her to Italy, where she fell in love with the glorious mysteries of Venice. Crystal chandeliers sparkled alongside impressively large Baroque mirrors, heavyweight leather-bound books lined the walls, while a Japanese Buddha rubbed shoulders with an African flute girl, and Dalí's *Wheat Ear* looked down from on high. The soft suede upholstery that Chanel found so calming was offset by walls lacquered in matt gold; lions, tarot cards and enamel boxes covered console tables, and in every corner stood eighteenth-century, Chinese coromandel screens. Adorned with birds of paradise, waterfalls and her favourite flower, the camellia, the screens obsessed her, and were continually moved around to create different spaces – and also to obscure the doors in her apartment – perhaps a reaction to her lifelong fear of abandonment.

26

THE LOGO

DATE: 1921

INSPIRATION: MANY COMPLEX INTERPRETATIONS

SIGNIFICANCE: GLOBAL BRANDING

The interlocking double Cs, which first appeared on bottles of N°5 perfume in 1921, have since become an instantly recognizable logo for Chanel's luxury brand. The visual shorthand of a graphic logo, so universally famous that it needs no further explanation, exemplifies a world of style and glamour, first personified by Coco Chanel herself.

The theories behind the provenance of Chanel's winning logo are numerous, and the inspiration for the simple design that turned out to be *so* successful may well have come from a combination of sources. The House of Chanel suggests that Catherine de' Medici used interlocking Cs as her monogram when she was Dauphine of France, and Chanel may have taken a liking to the historical reference. Alternatively, childhood memories from the circular patterns on the glass leaded windows of the Cistercian Abbey in Aubazine may have resonated. Or, as suggested by Justine Picardie in her book *Coco Chanel: The Legend & the Life*, the connected double Cs that face away from each other could represent a perpetual reminder of the handsome man she called her true love, Captain (or "Boy") Capel. Here was a man who believed in Chanel enough to financially support her early business ventures, but not enough to marry her because her social standing in society was too low, and the famous linked Cs perhaps suggest a couple inextricably bound together but pulling in different directions.

Stamped on to buttons, jewellery and purses, the logo has always signified the effortless allure of Coco Chanel.

27
BEADING

DATE: 1922
FABRICS: GLASS BEADS,
GOLD THREAD EMBROIDERY
PRODUCED BY: KITMIR ATELIER
SIGNIFICANCE: RUSSIAN CULTURE
INFLUENCED CHANEL

Through her romantic liaison with Grand Duke Dmitri Pavlovich, Chanel became entranced by the Slavic charm of Russia, sensing its untapped potential for commercialism. Influenced by her close friends Sergei Diaghilev and Igor Stravinsky, who had infiltrated the creative scene in Paris and were successfully presenting a fictional version of St Petersburg to Parisians, Chanel turned her attention to reinventing traditional Russian peasant clothing into something more contemporary.

Introduced to the duke's older sister, the Grand Duchess Maria Pavlova, who was looking for work, she commissioned her to decorate simple pieces of clothing with bugle beads and embroidery. Pavlova bought herself a sewing machine and quickly learned how to produce decorative machine embroidery, recruiting members of the expatriate community to join her atelier, which she called Kitmir. Sticking to a dark colour palette, Chanel reappropriated easy peasant pieces like the rustic-looking shift dress, workwear waistcoats and the *roubachka*-style blouse, which were then embellished with detailed beading and intricate stitching. The atelier specialized in labour-intensive decorative beadwork, executed by hand using tiny jet beads to create complex patterns on the fluid column dresses which became a recognized staple of Chanel in the mid '20s. The tubular flapper dresses that exemplified the Jazz Age were often entirely covered in crystal beads or sequins. With asymmetric hemlines, these dresses were designed for dancing, the glass beads dazzling on the dancefloor as non-stop parties became a regular pastime for Chanel's modern clientele.

28
PABLO PICASSO

DATE: 1922
INTRODUCED BY: JEAN COCTEAU AND PIERRE
REVERDY
RELATIONSHIP: FRIEND AND COLLABORATOR
SIGNIFICANCE: HIS ENDORSEMENT ELEVATED
HER ARTISTIC STATUS

Pablo Picasso and Chanel were part of the same set of artistic innovators in Paris, who, working within their own individual disciplines, instigated a revolution of modernity at the beginning of the twentieth century. Both had strong personalities and a vision of modernism that would be hugely influential in art and fashion; Picasso as one of the authors of abstract art, and Chanel as the couturière who brought about sweeping changes in contemporary dress.

Introduced by their mutual friend the poet Pierre Reverdy, they became friends as well as collaborators, working on many theatrical projects together, the first of which was for Jean Cocteau in 1922. Contributing to his avant-garde interpretation of the Greek tragedy *Antigone*, Picasso designed the sets and Chanel the costumes. The production was not well received – Picasso's masks and shields adorned with stylized Greek images were compared to shop windows during Mardi Gras – though Chanel herself was congratulated by the critics for her debut as costume designer. Years later Chanel revealed to the journalist Marcel Haedrich that although she was "fascinated" by Picasso, she was also filled with a "terrible fear": "I was a bit baffled by the sets he did for Stravinsky. I didn't really understand and wondered whether it was really beautiful." Picasso is widely known to have had a complicated relationship with women, once remarking: "For me there are only two types of women, goddesses and doormats." Chanel's artistic credibility guaranteed she fell into neither category, so their lifelong friendship endured.

29
MAKE-UP

DATE: 1924

CATALYST: HER PERSONAL BEAUTY NEEDS

MARKETING: BY 1924, PRODUCTS WERE
BRANDED WITH THE CC LOGO

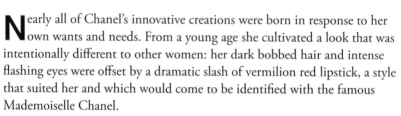

Nearly all of Chanel's innovative creations were born in response to her own wants and needs. From a young age she cultivated a look that was intentionally different to other women: her dark bobbed hair and intense flashing eyes were offset by a dramatic slash of vermilion red lipstick, a style that suited her and which would come to be identified with the famous Mademoiselle Chanel.

The prototype for her trademark red lipstick came in 1924 and was presented in an elegant ivory case, with production and packaging both quickly improved to create a lipstick that was marketed to customers in an elegant push-up case endorsed with a single C. That same year, she unveiled her first range of make-up, which included face powders and three lip colours. Unlike the rich society hostesses, whose beauty ideal of pale skin and coiffured hair reflected a life of wealth and inactivity, Chanel actively sought out physical activity and cultivated a healthy bronzed glow. Instinctively she sensed that her skin should be protected from the hours she spent in the sunshine and in 1932 she launched a small collection of suntan products. From the early 1930s Chanel expanded her range of beauty items, marketing moisturizing oils, perfumed talcum powder and fragranced soaps for her customers.

Fully aware that she was creating a covetable collection of merchandise, the chic black casing she presented with the distinctive white Chanel logo has since become the visual signature for a global beauty brand that provides superior scientific formulas for all its products.

30

LE TRAIN BLEU

DATE: 1924

VENUE: THÉÂTRE DES CHAMPS-ÉLYSÉES, PARIS

COLLABORATORS: JEAN COCTEAU, PABLO PICASSO,
HENRI LAURENS

PROFESSIONAL INVOLVEMENT: COSTUME
DESIGNER

Having previously created theatrical costumes for actresses including Cécile Sorel, Chanel agreed to provide costumes for a modern interpretation of the classical Greek tragedy *Antigone* for Jean Cocteau in 1922. She received rave reviews for her designs and was enrolled by Sergei Diaghilev to be part of the prodigious team of talent he recruited two years later for his production of *Le Train Bleu*, the night train that ferried wealthy passengers from Paris to the Riviera for a weekend of sunshine.

Premiered at the Théâtre des Champs-Élysées in June 1924, the ballet was a light-hearted look at the fashionable fads of the day, and included tennis players, golfing experts and bathers who expressed themselves through acrobatics and contemporary dance moves. Sets were designed by the cubist sculptor Henri Laurens, and Picasso was persuaded to let a highly skilled scenic artist Prince Schervachidze transpose his painting *Deux Femmes Courant sur la Plage* on to the front-of-house curtain for the production. Chanel was responsible for dressing the performers, but rather than creating an entirely new set of stage costumes for the production she dressed the cast in the stylish sportswear she was creating for her own customers. These knitted bathing costumes for men and women – striped jersey sweaters and drop-waist shift dresses – looked marvellous but proved impossible to dance in, as the loose fabric made it difficult for dancers to grasp each other securely in their routines. Impressed by the individual flair of the legendary French tennis player Suzanne Lenglen who always wore a stylish headband, Chanel designed an elegant version for the dancer Bronislava Nijinska.

31

"LE STYLE GARÇON"

DATE: 1925–29

ORIGINATED: PARIS

EXEMPLIFIED BY: SHORT HAIR, ANDROGYNOUS BODY

IN AMERICA: KNOWN AS "THE FLAPPER"

The shape of fashion was changing, with Chanel very much responsible for the new, slimmed down silhouette that had been identified as "le style garçon". The bestselling novel *La Garçonne* by Victor Margueritte caused a scandal when it appeared in July 1922. It detailed the story of Monique, a girl who dresses like a boy, has short bobbed hair, smokes cigarettes and is determined to make her own way in the world – a fictional tale that certainly resonated with parts of Chanel's own life story. Much of the couturière's innovative style came from a desire to flout existing conventions and accelerate the emancipation of women, but she was also influenced by the broader aesthetic changes of the Art Deco movement, which represented modernism in all forms of architecture and the decorative arts.

Chanel's tubular shift dresses, which were cleverly cut to avoid ugly side seams, required women to be as slim as a pin, and dieting became popular in an attempt to emulate the boyish body of Chanel. Hemlines were rising on her elaborately beaded flapper dresses, made to accommodate the hedonistic Roaring Twenties, a time when young people from both sides of the Atlantic rebelled against pre-war attitudes, with a perpetual round of cocktails and dancing. Chanel's relationship with the Duke of Westminster, whom she met in 1923, was also influential, as she reappropriated sporting jackets and trousers from his male wardrobe into her collections, reinforcing the success of "le style garçon".

32

GARDENIA

DATE: 1925
CREATED BY: GABRIELLE
CHANEL / ERNEST BEAUX
INGREDIENTS: GARDENIA, JASMINE, MIMOSA

The sales of Chanel's first foray into the perfume market proved she had the Midas touch – with the invention of Nº5, she had created an immediate bestseller – and the couturière was keen to capitalize on her success.

In 1925 she presented a fresh new perfume called Gardenia, which was advertised using the strapline "Youthful Gardenia" and evocative copy that spoke of a romantic vision of flower-filled gardens in the south of France, under moonlight and with sound of music in the distance. The floral scent, presented like Nº5 in a modern pharmaceutical bottle with square stopper and stylish graphic labelling, was created in the perfume laboratory of the esteemed perfumer Ernest Beaux. Working from his headquarters in Grasse, Beaux was appointed the first chief perfumer of Les Parfums Chanel, the company set up to produce all Chanel's future perfumes.

The concept for Gardenia may come from the purity of Chanel's favourite flower, the camellia, a bloom famed for its symmetrical beauty but absolutely odourless. In contrast, the gardenia, with its large white petals that so closely resemble those of the camellia, produces an extremely sensual fragrance that makes it a perfect choice for the perfume industry. The original formula for the green floral perfume contained a narcissus base with a fresh green note of styrallyl acetate, mimosa and gardenia, resulting in "a fresh and sensual nectar".

33

THE LITTLE BLACK DRESS

DATE: 1926

STYLE: BLOUSON SHEATH DRESS

FABRIC: CRÊPE DE CHINE

UPDATED VERSIONS WORN BY: EVERY RED CARPET,

A-LIST STAR

When American *Vogue* first published an illustration of Chanel's new black crêpe de Chine dress in October 1926, they heralded her triumph as "a frock that all the world will wear".

Alluding to the success of Ford's mass-produced, Model T automobile, they dubbed the streamlined simplicity of her design "the Ford dress" – and their prediction that it would become a uniform staple which women everywhere would want to own has proven to be remarkably astute. The boat-necked, long-sleeved dress was adorned only with a deep-set, pleated V from shoulder to waist, mirrored with similar detailing in the straight skirt that grazed the knee, creating an understated elegance. Chanel had inadvertently coined the term "LBD", and she would forever be associated with this original version of her Little Black Dress, which went on to inspire a multitude of variations, becoming an iconic must-have in contemporary fashion.

The inspiration to launch a range of radically simple black sheath dresses in 1926 has never been fully explained, although the misery of mourning her lover Boy Capel's death has been suggested and she was also vociferously contemptuous of the flamboyant couturier Paul Poiret's gaudy colour schemes. He responded by labelling her understated minimalism as "poverty de luxe". Chanel was the first designer to utilize black materials for both day and evening wear, from the late 1910s onward, creating practical day dresses in wool and marocain, and using both matt and shiny silk satins and crêpes to create chic evening dresses that did not require additional embellishment.

34
LA PAUSA

DATE: 1928
LOCATION: ROQUEBRUNE-CAP-MARTIN, CÔTE D'AZUR
ARCHITECT: ROBERT STREITZ
GUESTS: JEAN COCTEAU, SALVADOR DALÍ,
DUKE OF WESTMINSTER

In 1928 Chanel bought a sun-kissed plot of land with magnificent views of the sparkling Mediterranean coastline and set about building herself a grand estate. With a clear plan of what she had in mind, Chanel hired the young architect Robert Streitz to create an impressive central villa with seven bedrooms, as well as guest villas set in the grounds, to accommodate friends. Inspired by the understated beauty of the monastery at Aubazine, where she spent her childhood, Chanel insisted that Streitz visit the twelfth-century convent to use elements of the abbey as a basis for La Pausa. Most notably, a sweeping stone staircase (similar to the one she climbed every day as a child) was built as the focal point of the entrance hall, around an open-plan central courtyard, with ecclesiastically styled arched windows.

Chanel was a demanding boss, who wanted to approve every decision regarding the construction of the house and gardens of her new Riviera home, and once a month she would travel down from Paris on the night train to Monte Carlo, to keep an eye on its progress. The beautiful villa was finally ready in 1929 and had cost Chanel several million francs to build. The house was meticulously styled, with a restrained colour palette of softly muted shades, and during the summer months Chanel hosted some of the most talked about parties in Europe, with a guest list that included the celebrated ballet dancer and choreographer Serge Lifar, Jean Cocteau, Salvador and Gala Dalí, and her lover the Duke of Westminster. Chanel sold La Pausa in 1953.

35
WHITE DRESSES

DATE: 1930s
FABRICS: SILK, SATIN, TULLE
CATALYST: WALL STREET CRASH
SIGNIFICANCE: FEMININITY
REPLACES ANDROGYNY

Having successfully brought the Little Black Dress into mainstream fashion from 1926 onward, Chanel was as eager to exploit the potential of white, a colour she associated with the purity of her convent uniform from her days at the Aubazine monastery. She was quick to recognize the showstopping impact of a glamorous all-white evening gown, telling her friend the writer Paul Morand in 1946, "I have said that black had everything. White too. They have an absolute beauty. It is perfect harmony. Dress women in white or black at a ball: they are the only ones you see."

The Wall Street Crash in 1929 threw America into a financial depression, which perversely acted as a catalyst to Parisian designers to explore a period of high-octane luxury extravagance. White and cream satin dominated Chanel's collection of glitzy evening gowns in the early 1930s. Focusing on a single dazzling colour, coupled with her innate desire for simplicity, resulted in eveningwear that was dramatic but never ostentatious. A decorative bow on the bodice or a low-cut revealing back were trademark characteristics of this period, and although Chanel had ventured into slightly more feminine styles in the 1930s, occasionally adding a ruffle or two or some lace details, she continued to embrace modernism and rejected the eccentric gimmicks of her rival Elsa Schiaparelli.

White remained a showstopper on the catwalk, and Chanel included a series of stunning white cocktail dresses in her collections in the mid '50s.

36

THE BRETON

DATE: 1930
SOURCE: WORKWEAR INSPIRED
SIGNIFICANCE: CLASSLESS APPEAL

Early success for Chanel came from her ability to recognize essentially good design in the functional uniforms of the working men she saw around her. The French navy posted in Brittany were the first to adopt the striped Breton top as a utilitarian piece of warm clothing: a boat neck allowed sailors to dress quickly, and horizontal stripes would be spotted easily against an expanse of ocean if anyone fell overboard.

The first photographs of Chanel wearing a classic Breton striped T-shirt, tucked stylishly into high-waisted loose trousers, come from 1930, when she was on holiday in her villa on the Côte d'Azur, but her instincts to reappropriate other aspects of the working clothes she saw on the fishermen in Deauville had come much earlier. In 1913 she was inspired to create her first *blouson marinière* – a loose-fitting pullover blouse for women that simply slipped on over the head, did not require a corset to be worn, and proved to be a big hit with her customers.

Chic nautical stripes remained a recurring theme in much of Chanel's work, prominent in her 1917 nautical collection, and also endorsed by the bohemian crowd of artists she collaborated with in the 1920s. Pablo Picasso was regularly photographed in his studio wearing the striped Breton top of the traditional sailor. Inspiration from the colour palette of Chanel's early endorsement of the Breton stripe also proved to be enduring, as crisp navy and white remained a winning combination.

37

HOLLYWOOD

DATE: 1931
LOCATION: CALIFORNIA
OUTCOME: COSTUME DESIGNER FOR THREE FILMS

In response to the Wall Street Crash of 1929, the wisecracking Hollywood producer Samuel Goldwyn conceived a simple but costly plan, to distract millions of employed Americans from their daily misery. If he could get Chanel on board as a celebrity costume designer, he could provide the public with a plot line of escapist fantasy and first-class Parisian fashion, while

simultaneously ensuring that some of her stylish allure rubbed off on the unrefined tastes of his leading ladies, whose vulgar extravagances were at odds with public opinion. Through their mutual friend Dmitri Pavlovich, Goldwyn stage-managed an introduction in Monaco, and after much persuasion and the promise of a million-dollar contract, Chanel agreed to travel to California to see what the movie industry could offer her.

With Misia Sert alongside, she sailed to New York in April 1931 and then journeyed onward by train to Los Angeles Union Station, where she was greeted by a welcome party that included the screen royals Greta Garbo and Marlene Dietrich. On arrival, the world-famous couturière made it very clear that she would *not* neglect her own business, would not stay to design costumes (the actresses would travel to Paris) and would *not* be subordinate to the star system. Chanel's relationship with Hollywood was short-lived; none of the three films she worked on (*Palmy Days*, 1931; *The Greeks Had a Word for Them*, 1932; *Tonight or Never*, 1931) were huge box office hits, although her costumes for Gloria Swanson were critically acclaimed and her friendship with Goldwyn survived.

38
BOWS

DATE: 1930s
FABRIC: GROSGRAIN, SATIN, SILK
SIGNIFICANCE: FEMININE TOUCH TO
MASCULINE AESTHETIC

Although Chanel built her early reputation on understated elegance, she often included a decorative bow as a nod to femininity, in an otherwise clean-cut masculine silhouette.

During her career as a modiste, she embellished the stark Breton boaters she bought from Galeries Lafayette with a simple grosgrain ribbon tied into a bow at the back, a reaction against the frilly plumage of the Belle Époque style. Photographs of Chanel in 1908 at Chateau de Royallieu, the estate owned by Étienne Balsan, show her wearing cropped trousers and a plain white shirt, embellished with a simple black tape tied loosely into a bow at her neck – a look she continued to present with her androgynous 1950s jersey suits, worn with neat ribbon bow ties.

As her fame and influence as a fashion icon grew, the bow became a signature of the House of Chanel, and she punctuated many of her collections with assorted bows in an abundance of different forms. In the 1930s Chanel surprised everyone by producing a stunning range of lavish evening dresses that featured bows, either as a focal point on the bodice or placed decoratively on the back, accentuating the deep V of a backless gown. Her cotton piqué suits from this time are offset by the addition of an oversized pussycat bow blouse, a design trait she perpetuated with her 1960s' classic tweed suits and silk blouses. In 1932, she even included the precious bow motif in her famous exhibition Bijoux de Diamants, creating imaginative pieces that captivated the public with their graceful beauty.

39

PAUL IRIBE

DATE: 1931

PROFESSION: ILLUSTRATOR, SET AND COSTUME
DESIGNER

RELATIONSHIP: POTENTIAL HUSBAND

At the age of 50, Chanel, the most famous couturière in the world, found herself at the centre of circling rumours that she would finally submit to a man and marry for the first time – to the French illustrator Paul Iribe. Her exact contemporary, Iribe had a long and illustrious career behind him, having found fame at the age of 23, when he produced his own satirical magazine *Le Témoin*. The fluidity of his draftsmanship won him renown, and the couturier Paul Poiret commissioned him in 1908 to create an album of stylized drawings of his work. *Les Robes de Paul Poiret racontées par Paul Iribe* was highly praised, but a change of direction saw Iribe cross the Atlantic to Hollywood, where he was championed as a set and costume designer by the genius film producer Cecil B DeMille.

As a member of Misia Sert's bohemian art set, Chanel was introduced to Iribe in Paris in 1931 and went on to collaborate with him on her extravagant *Bijoux de Diamants* exhibition, where he successfully interpreted her ideas into fully formed designs. Although the "chubby Basque" (as Paul Poiret referred to him) had strong political leanings and was not her usual type, the couple embarked on a passionate love affair, which she hoped would provide her with lasting happiness. In August 1935, Iribe visited Chanel at her holiday retreat on the Riviera, where he suffered a heart attack playing tennis and dropped dead at her feet. She did not recover from this second tragedy in her personal life.

40

BIJOUX DE DIAMANTS

DATE: NOVEMBER 1932
LOCATION: RUE DU FAUBOURG SAINT-HONORÉ
LANDMARK: FIRST DIAMOND JEWELLERY COLLECTION
SIGNIFICANCE: ENTRANCE FEE DONATED TO CHARITY

At nearly 50 years old, having championed fake gemstones and artificial pearls throughout her career, Chanel surprised everyone in Paris by presenting a spectacular exhibition of diamond jewellery, displayed in the ground floor of her own eighteenth-century apartment on the rue du Faubourg Saint-Honoré. With very little previous experience of working with precious stones, Chanel was approached by the International Guild of Diamond Merchants with a proposal to create a range of diamond jewellery. It would be displayed in a lavish exhibition designed to boost interest in precious stones, as sales had dwindled due to the Depression.

Working in collaboration with the French designer Paul Iribe, Chanel produced a stunning collection of stylish graphic jewellery based on five basic themes: celestial bodies, bows, fringes, feathers and geometric patterns. With discreet clasps and invisible mounts, several of the pieces executed in platinum and white diamonds were designed to be multifunctional: a tiara could be worn as a necklace, earrings could be converted into hairclips, and the famous Comète choker, a glittering star with a shooting trail of diamonds, simply clung to the nape of the neck without any fastenings at all. The exhibition required armed guards to protect the priceless gems, and public demand to see what Chanel had created was unprecedented. The exhibition attracted thousands of visitors over a two-week period, all paying an entrance fee of 20 francs and the proceeds being donated to two charities, Assistance Privée à la Classe Moyenne and Société de la Charité Maternelle de Paris.

41

MARLENE DIETRICH

DATE: 1933
CHAMPIONED: ANDROGYNOUS STYLE
WORE: CHANEL SERGE WOOL TROUSER SUIT

In the 1930s Hollywood stars projected an unattainable glamour that the rest of the world looked to emulate, slavishly following the fashion and beauty trends set on the silver screen.

German-born Marlene Dietrich, famous for her razor-sharp cheekbones and plucked-to-nothing eyebrows, was a pioneer of androgynous fashion, often appearing in publicity shots dressed entirely in menswear, and even appearing at the premiere of her 1932 film *The Sign of the Cross* in a man's tuxedo, wing-collared shirt and bow tie, with a soft trilby hat and mannish leather brogues. Challenging gender stereotypes in Hollywood, in the same way that Chanel popularized a new trend for appropriating items from a male wardrobe, she scandalized the public, who were initially shocked by the notion of flouting conventional gender norms.

With broad shoulders and narrow hips, Dietrich was well suited to Chanel's casual tailoring, and in 1933 appeared looking fabulously modern in a Chanel single-breasted grey serge suit, worn with an understated turtleneck sweater and French beret. With Dietrich and Chanel as stylish role models, the notion of androgynous dressing, which encouraged women to wear clothes that were practical as well as elegant, became more mainstream. Dietrich's status as film star and iconic trendsetter even led to department stores advertising "Marlene Mannish Styles".

42

THE RITZ

DATE: 1935
LOCATION: PLACE VENDÔME, PARIS
SIGNIFICANCE: CHANEL LIVED AND DIED AT
THE RITZ
FAMOUS GUESTS: MARCEL PROUST, ERNEST
HEMINGWAY, F SCOTT FITZGERALD

Located in the heart of Paris, and overlooking Place Vendôme and Napoleon's famous Column, is one of the most glamorous hotels in the world, regarded by Chanel as her second home for more than 30 years. The couturière lived at The Ritz from 1935 onward, her most iconic suite of rooms being those she occupied from 1935–40, on the third floor.

She always retained a luxurious apartment above her flagship store, for entertaining, but did not sleep there. After a long day's work in the atelier, Chanel would simply cross the road, enter The Ritz through the back rue Cambon entrance, and ascend to her rooms, where her precious scissors were placed on a dressing table beside her bed. Chanel took her place at the same table in the dining room each night, positioned where she could be seen and gossiped about, but could also critically assess the arrival of other guests. During the Second World War, The Ritz stayed open despite being requisitioned by the Germans who occupied Paris. High-ranking officials came to an unexpectedly amicable arrangement with the owner, agreeing to keep the Vendôme side of the hotel for officers while allowing civilians to occupy the rue Cambon buildings.

Having initially fled for safety as the German army marched into Paris, Chanel soon returned to the capital, only to find the swastika flying high above the Eiffel Tower and her suite at The Ritz commandeered by Nazi officers. Unperturbed, she agreed to downsize and continued to live in a small room at the back of the hotel for the duration of the war.

43
THE MALTESE CUFF

DATE: 1937

MATERIALS: COLOURED BAROQUE STONES, ENAMEL

DESIGNED BY: GABRIELLE CHANEL
(REALIZED BY FULCO DI VERDURA)

Fulco Santostefano della Cerda, Duke of Verdura, the aristocratic Sicilian more commonly known as Fulco, was to assist on the design of what became known as some of Chanel's most iconic pieces of jewellery. Introduced to each other by mutual acquaintances Diana Vreeland and Cole Porter, the couple developed a great friendship alongside their working relationship, sharing a passion for Byzantine mosaics and artistic treasures. In the Basilica of San Vitale, Ravenna, Italy, they were particularly impressed by the Byzantine mosaic of Empress Theodora. Chanel and Verdura also shared a love of theatrical statement jewellery, both of them eschewing traditional pieces with discreet jewels and settings, and instead favouring bold dazzling colour in the form of Byzantine designs featuring large, semi-precious gemstones.

The chunky cuff bracelets that Chanel wore on each arm, and was rarely photographed without, were designed by Verdura, at Chanel's request, for her personal collection. The Maltese cross was a symbol remembered from her childhood at Aubazine, where it appeared as part of the flooring design and in other architectural features. Made from white enamel that eventually became chipped from everyday wear and tear, the cuffs were not identical, each one having a unique setting that mixed precious and semi-precious gemstones like emerald cabochons, topaz, citrine and tourmaline. Variations on the distinctive black and white Maltese cross cuffs, made by expert jewellers, became a House of Chanel staple that helped elevate her passion for statement jewellery into a commercial trend for haute-couture customers.

44
GYPSY STYLE

DATE: 1939
FABRICS: SILK, COTTON, RAYON
COLOURS: RED, WHITE, BLUE
SIGNIFICANCE: LINGERIE TROPES AS OUTERWEAR

In response to the imminent threats of war that hung heavily over Europe, Chanel seemed determined to show the world her patriotic loyalty and produced a collection of stunning, gypsy-style dresses in the vibrant colours of the French Tricolour. At a time of uncertainty, she provided a form of escapism, presenting a collection that catered for society women who were still attending grand parties, dancing through the night with roses in their hair, wearing a gypsy gown – a look that alluded to more carefree, innocent times.

Chanel was the designer who had done so much to strip away the excessive decoration and fancy frills of a previous era, so the flamboyant beauty of her dresses, with their crinoline-shaped overskirts and extravagant puffed sleeves, took everyone by surprise. The spirited colour palette replaced her regular muted tones, while the romantic gypsy silhouette, which consisted of a short bodice with frothy layers of under- and overskirts adorned with lace ruffles at the hem, were unlike any of her previous creations. Fearless in her desire to explore new avenues of creativity, Chanel used techniques of modern lingerie to produce broderie anglaise camisoles that fitted closely to the body and were designed to be seen through a high-necked layer of diaphanous tulle. Blurring the line between provocation and modesty, creating underwear that was visible as outerwear, Chanel proved yet again that she was a fashion pioneer.

45

MARILYN MONROE

DATE: APRIL 1952
CIRCUMSTANCE: INTERVIEW WITH *LIFE* MAGAZINE
FAMOUS QUOTE: "I ONLY WEAR CHANEL Nº5"
SIGNIFICANCE: BOOSTED WORLDWIDE SALES OF
THE PERFUME

When Tinseltown's sexiest blonde bombshell met with the chic Parisian style of Coco Chanel, it could only ever be good for business on both sides of the Atlantic. When Marilyn Monroe appeared on the front cover of *Life* magazine in April 1952 she was at the start of her career, not yet famous as a sex goddess with a fragile vulnerability that would make her so bankable to an international audience. *Life's* feature "The Talk of Hollywood" revealed for the first time the actress's preference for Chanel's distinctive perfume. She divulged that when asked the question, "Marilyn, what do you wear to bed?", she answered "I only wear Chanel Nº5". A few years later she posed for a series of photographs for *Modern Screen*, seductively wrapped up in white satin sheets with a bottle of Nº5 on her bedside table.

In 1955, in an attempt to break away from Hollywood and establish herself as a serious actress in New York, Monroe agreed to spend several days with a reportage photographer Ed Feingersh, who would capture her in relaxed, spontaneous settings, including taking the New York subway and drinking coffee at a corner deli. A stylish black-and-white image from this session of photo realism shows Monroe dressed up and getting ready to go out, head thrown back in ecstasy, clutching her favourite bottle of Nº5 to her chest. It was a powerful image, too good to waste, and decades later it has been used in many books and magazines to celebrate the iconic pairing of Monroe and Chanel Nº5.

46

CHAINS

DATE: 1954
INSPIRATION: MEMORIES OF HER EARLY LIFE
MATERIALS: GILT AND BRASS
PURPOSE: BOTH DECORATIVE AND PRACTICAL

Much of the iconography that has become synonymous with the House of Chanel can be traced directly back to the personal history of the couturière's early life. Her continual use of gilt chains took many different forms, becoming a recurring theme in her collections, either as statement costume jewellery or utilized in a practical capacity.

Chanel was a skilful stylist who played the part of a fashionable arbiter of taste; leading by example, she effortlessly influenced the habits of her clientele. In 1937 she posed for a portrait by the German photographer Horst P Horst, who captured a romantic vision of her lounging on a satin armchair, a handful of unmissably large gilt chains hanging casually over her shoulder. Later she would throw "gold" chains around the waist of her elegant suits, hanging keys or medals on to the loops, reminiscent of the belts worn by the nuns who had looked after her at Aubazine. The interwoven leather and chain strap which made the 2.55 handbag so practical was inspired by the horse bridles and harnesses she used for riding, during the happy times spent in the stables at Chateau de Royallieu. Chanel once spoke of an old friend from her childhood who kept the hem of her skirt from brushing the floor by the addition of a metal chain, and said: "Perhaps that's where my fondness for chains comes from." It was an idea she copied successfully many years later, using tiny chains concealed discreetly on the inside of her jackets and skirts, to weight the fabric and ensure a perfect hang when worn.

47
THE SUIT

DATE: 1954
WORN THEN BY: GRACE KELLY, ELIZABETH TAYLOR,
JACKIE KENNEDY
WORN NOW BY: ANNA MOUGLALIS,
PENÉLOPE CRUZ, SOFIA COPPOLA

Although Chanel had been creating easy-to-wear suits that consisted of loose cardigan jackets and fluid skirts from her early days in Deauville, it was not until her comeback, at the age of 70, that she produced the elegant suit which would eventually define her legacy. The success of Christian Dior's restrictive New Look horrified her, and the classic suits she produced in 1954 visibly demonstrated her underlying principle of womenswear, to prioritize comfort and ease. The silhouette remained balanced, comfortable as well as practical, although significantly more tailored than previously, and it was the unique styling details that Chanel started to add that would elevate her suits to iconic fashion status.

American women were the first to recognize the significance of Chanel's creativity, offering the suit as a contemporary uniform that could be adopted for all occasions. Jackets were soft and boxy to allow freedom of movement; the fit of the armhole was essential, and Chanel spent hours re-fitting sleeves in search of perfection. Silk blouses and jacket linings were often made from the same fabric; the simple collarless neckline signalled modernity; pockets were designed for practical use, not just for show; and decorative gilt buttons were matched with flawless buttonholes. Chanel used braid to finish the raw edges of a jacket, sometimes adding the same trim to cuffs, collars and pockets, and to ensure a jacket hung properly she added a fine chain to the hem of the lining. The enduring success of her signature suits consolidated her place in fashion history.

48

2.55 HANDBAG

DATE: FEBRUARY 1955
MATERIALS: GILT CHAIN STRAP, QUILTED LEATHER
OWNED BY: ANNA WINTOUR, PHOEBE PHILO,
SOFIA COPPOLA

Decades before the concept of a designer handbag symbolized the visual status of a luxury couture house, Chanel created the classic 2.55 quilted bag, based entirely, like the majority of her design innovations, on her own personal desire for practical solutions to everyday problems. "I was fed up with holding my purses in my hands and losing them," she said.

A long gilt chain and leather strap to be worn over the shoulder and a secure twist-lock, known as the Mademoiselle Lock, to keep the contents safe, as well as several useful compartments inside the bag (one designed specifically to carry the red lipstick she was never seen without), are the now instantly recognizable features of this coveted item. Named after the date of its launch in February, the second month of 1955, the bag quickly became one of Chanel's signature pieces, to add to her existing iconography. Harnessing design inspiration from snapshots of her own past, the lambskin leather chosen for both its strength and suppleness was meticulously overstitched, producing a diamond matelassé effect reminiscent of the quilted fabric worn by the stable boys she learned to ride with at Étienne Balsan's estate. Horse bridles and reins are most likely to have inspired the distinctive metal chain woven through with strips of polished leather, and the deep burgundy lining is thought to have been a reference to the habits worn at the monastery in Aubazine. Chanel created three different sizes of the bag. Each size could be realized in soft leather for day wear or silk jersey for evening.

49

TWO-TONE SHOES

DATE: 1957
MATERIALS: KIDSKIN LEATHER, BLACK SATIN
STYLE: TWO-TONE SLINGBACK
WORN BY: GINA LOLLOBRIGIDA, ROMY SCHNEIDER,
CATHERINE DENEUVE

Although Chanel's famous two-tone slingback shoes were introduced into her collection in 1957, there is evidence of the couturière wearing her own version of two-tone footwear at an earlier date. In a photograph taken with the principal dancer of the Ballets Russes, Serge Lifar, in about 1937, Chanel sports a prototype of her famous shoe, consisting of a neutral-coloured sandal with a neat black toecap. In much the same way that a desire

for practicality and simplicity ruled other creative innovations in her career, the thought process behind the elegant two-tone shoe was very pragmatic. A shoe made entirely out of nude kidskin leather would show every scuff mark and speck of dirt, but the clever addition of a contrasting dark toe would help to hide the marks and keep the shoes looking smarter for longer.

With the help of Raymond Massaro, the shoemaker supplying the House, Chanel conceived the idea for a beige shoe that would visually lengthen the leg and complement the skin, while simultaneously the use of a black, slightly square toecap would deceive the eye and foreshorten the size of the foot. Stiletto heels were fashionable in the '50s, but Chanel wanted women to feel comfortable, and opted for an elastic slingback strap and small but sturdy heel (just 6 cm/2¼ in), which provided enough of a height boost without compromising the ability to walk properly. Inspiration behind her elegant two-tone shoes may have come from the black-and-white wing-tipped sports shoes worn by her aristocratic English friends on the golf course in the 1930s.

50

ELIZABETH TAYLOR

DATE: 1960s

WORE: BOUCLÉ TWEED SUIT AND
CHANEL HANDBAG

SIGNIFICANCE: ENDORSEMENT BY
WORLD-FAMOUS ACTRESS

Following her comeback collection, which launched on 5 March 1954, Chanel's reputation soared as the best-dressed women of the world made a pilgrimage to her door, hoping the inclusion of an iconic suit in their wardrobes would impart an aura of elusive French style. At the height of her fame, when she could pick from the best designers in the world, Elizabeth Taylor chose to wear haute couture by Chanel, and would regularly visit 31 rue Cambon for fittings in the large reception room on the first floor. In the early '60s Taylor was regularly photographed with her fourth husband Eddie Fisher, dressed head to toe in classic Chanel suits, carrying the 2.55 handbag and wearing the signature boater, the ultimate stylish uniform for a glamorous film star.

In many ways the two women had little in common: Chanel favoured a neutral colour palette, enjoyed a disciplined working routine and strictly controlled her diet, whereas Taylor had an exuberant zest for life that manifested itself in her personal style. She loved bold colours, glitzy fabrics and statement jewellery, and was not afraid to stamp her own identity on an outfit with mismatched accessories. Unlike Chanel, who espoused the "less is more" school of dressing and thought a woman should always take a good look at herself in the mirror and take one thing off before she left the house, Taylor took a different approach. She was unapologetic about her love of expensive jewellery and would often overload an outfit with rings, brooches and bracelets, as well as wearing jewellery in her hair. Taylor combined her love of maximalism with Chanel's chic Parisian designs to glorious effect.

51

JACKIE KENNEDY

DATE: 22 NOVEMBER 1963

WORE: PINK CHANEL SUIT

LOCATION: DALLAS, TEXAS

LEGACY: IMAGES OF THE FIRST LADY CIRCULATED

AROUND THE GLOBE

Mrs John F Kennedy was just one of the rich and famous clients who flocked to rue Cambon, becoming a Chanel couture customer between 1955 and 1958. The wife of the American president was expected to wear only home-grown couture, but the global success of Chanel's stylish suit, an international byword for understated elegance in high society, made it an obvious choice for official duties.

When JFK set out to Dallas on 22 November 1963, Jackie Kennedy was by his side wearing a Chanel suit, created for her at 31 rue Cambon. The suit was not purchased by the first lady herself – a friend was sent to the atelier with Mrs Kennedy's measurements in hand. The look, taken from Chanel's autumn/winter 1961 haute-couture collection, was one of her favourites, and she had already been seen at official engagements wearing the vivid pink, bouclé jacket with navy taffeta trim and decorative gilt buttons, with matching skirt and pillbox hat. The Kennedys were travelling side by side through the streets of Dallas, in an open-top Lincoln Continental, when bullet shots aimed at the president rang out, killing him instantly. Splattered with blood and gore from her husband's fatal injuries, Jackie Kennedy refused to change out of her bloodstained suit, saying: "I want them to see what they have done to Jack." The suit was never cleaned and, along with the stockings and accessories she wore that day, was put into an acid-free box at the National Archives, Maryland.

52

COCO ON
BROADWAY

DATE: DECEMBER 1969
LOCATION: MARK HELLINGER THEATRE, BROADWAY
STAGE SETS AND COSTUMES BY: CECIL BEATON
DURATION: 329 PERFORMANCES

The Danish-American producer Frederick Brisson first approached Chanel to discuss an adaptation of her life in the form of a play or a film as early as 1956, but it took many years of protracted negotiations before his vision became a reality. The synopsis for *Coco*, the musical, centred around the French couturière's comeback in the early '50s after years of retirement.

Chanel approved of the first-class team of creatives who were to provide music and lyrics, as both André Previn and Alan Jay Lerner were established in their fields, but she was vexed that the story focused on her later life, rather than her early successes, and even more annoyed to discover that she would not be required to provide costumes for her own life story. Instead Cecil Beaton, who had already won two Oscars for his outstanding film costumes, was chosen to design the stage wardrobe for *Coco*. The producers felt Chanel's original outfits would be too subtle (dull) for the theatre and that Beaton could produce costumes capturing the essence of Chanel while offering the additional wow factor needed to entertain the audience.

Katherine Hepburn was chosen to play the title role, and looked stylish in her Beaton costumes, but she had never sung or danced before and did not attempt a French accent. Chanel planned to attend the opening night in New York but at the last minute changed her mind. The reviews were lukewarm, though the show was popular with the public and ran for just under a year.

53
CHANEL Nº19

DATE: 1970
PERFUMER: HENRI ROBERT
INGREDIENTS: IRIS ROOT, MAY ROSE, JASMINE
SIGNIFICANCE: NAMED AFTER CHANEL'S BIRTHDATE

Upon the retirement of Ernest Beaux in 1954, a new "nose" took over at Parfums Chanel in 1955. Henri Robert, a Grasse native, had worked as a successful perfumer for Coty, before working alongside Beaux for Chanel and eventually succeeding him as master perfumer. Robert was responsible for the last perfume Chanel ever launched and personally wore, called Nº19.

In her late 80s, Chanel set out to create a brand-new perfume. What she created was stamped with a unique identity, offering a sensory aroma that was diametrically different to Nº5 and feisty enough to appeal in the changing times. The name was chosen to commemorate Chanel's own birthday, 19 August. The packaging was strikingly familiar to that of its famous predecessor, but the woody ingredients produced something distinctly more daring than the heady warmth of Nº5. The distillation of ingredients was a complex process as the fragrance was primarily built around ground iris root, which requires a drying out period of several years, allowing the scent to develop before it can be turned into a workable liquid.

Nº19 was cool and green in appearance, including many springtime blossoms – May rose, jasmine, lily of the valley – in the perfectly balanced formula. The distinct green notes come from the aromatic plant galbanum, while the soft powdery notes are attributed to the addition of *Iris pallida* (sweet iris). Chanel died a year after Nº19 was launched, and although it has never achieved the heady success of Nº5, it has built up a fanbase of customers who have remained loyal to the fragrance.

54

10 JANUARY 1971

VENUE: BEDROOM
LOCATION: THE RITZ, PLACE VENDÔME
SIGNIFICANCE: THE HOUSE OF CHANEL LAY
DORMANT FOR 12 YEARS
FINAL RESTING PLACE: LAUSANNE, SWITZERLAND

During the course of a 60-year career, Chanel achieved both fame and fortune. In later years, without the distraction of family or a special man in her life, Chanel became an obsessive workaholic, channelling her time and energy into the House of Chanel, her constant companion. With most of her creative collaborators gone, she lived an increasingly solitary existence, working at rue Cambon six days a week with a loyal retinue of staff, and sleeping in her spartan rooms at The Ritz, where a butler and maid took care of her. Despite her advancing years, her desire to present one more winning collection never waned, her work ethic as relentless as when she started out.

Chanel died on Sunday, 10 January 1971 in her bed at The Ritz, aged 88. Her funeral, attended by all the great Parisian couturiers eager to pay their respects, took place at L'église de la Madeleine, next to rue Cambon, and her final resting place is in Lausanne, Switzerland. Her tomb bears simply her name, Gabrielle Chanel, and the date of her birth and death, under a headstone embossed with five lion heads. Chanel had become an iconic figure, recognized throughout the world for both her personal style and contribution to fashion. Fifty years on, her position as the most influential designer of the twentieth century remains unchallenged.

55

KARL
LAGERFELD

DATE: 1983

OCCUPATION: DESIGNER FOR CHLOÉ, KRIZIA, FENDI

IMPACT: CREATIVE DIRECTOR OF CHANEL FOR OVER
30 YEARS

When the German-born designer Karl Lagerfeld arrived at the House of Chanel in 1983, 12 years after the death of the legendary Grande Mademoiselle, he knew he was undertaking a seemingly impossible task. Despite the longstanding reputation of Chanel, the couturière who had single-handedly forced fashion to change direction and provided women with a contemporary wardrobe appropriate for an evolving society, the couture house had gone into a decline since Chanel's death. This was a brand still heavily entrenched in its own back catalogue of tweed suits, suitable, as Lagerfeld told *The Daily Telegraph*, only for "Parisian doctors' wives". But Lagerfeld accepted the challenge, and set about representing the personal codes of Chanel for a new generation of women.

From his first presentation, which took place in the rue Cambon salon in January 1983, Lagerfeld was able to reinvent the famous signatures of Chanel, taking points of reference from her most iconic motifs and pieces; the camellia, quilting, chains, pearls and LBDs were all given a makeover by "Kaiser Karl". Luxury tweeds edged in lurex, extravagant costume jewellery, oversized bows and playful use of trompe l'oeil chains all became part of his updated iconography for the label, and the ubiquitous interlocking double C logo was boldly stamped on to every type of merchandise, from moon boots to surfboards. Successfully tweaking proportions and silhouettes, favouring opulent fabrics and embracing deconstructivism, Lagerfeld found a new young audience for Chanel. Following Lagerfeld's death at the age of 85 in 2019, Virginie Viard has continued to reinterpret Gabrielle Chanel's codes in the fashion collections of the House of Chanel.

INDEX

FIN